Shall We Dance?

IRISH DANCE

by Wendy Hinote Lanier

FOCUS
READERS

www.focusreaders.com

Focus Readers is distributed by North Star Editions:
sales@northstareditions.com | 888-417-0195

Produced for Focus Readers by Red Line Editorial.

Photographs ©: DarkBird/Shutterstock Images, cover, 1, 10–11; salajean/Shutterstock Images, 4–5; Zvonimir Atletic/Shutterstock Images, 6, 14–15, 26; Vsevolod33/Shutterstock Images, 9; klazing/iStockphoto, 13; Dominic Lipinski/Press Association/URN: 19556296/ AP Images, 17, 29; 279photo Studio/Shutterstock Images, 18; Max Topchii/Shutterstock Images, 20–21; Niall Carson/Press Association/URN: 16064608/AP Images, 22–23; Kobby Dagan/Shutterstock Images, 25

ISBN
978-1-63517-275-1 (hardcover)
978-1-63517-340-6 (paperback)
978-1-63517-470-0 (ebook pdf)
978-1-63517-405-2 (hosted ebook)

Library of Congress Control Number: 2017935119

Printed in the United States of America
Mankato, MN
June, 2017

About the Author

Wendy Hinote Lanier is a native Texan and former elementary teacher who writes and speaks for children and adults on a variety of topics. She is the author of more than 20 books for children and young people. Some of her favorite people are dogs.

TABLE OF CONTENTS

CHAPTER 1

WHAT IS IRISH DANCE?

A dancer takes the stage. Then two more join him. Their arms stay at their sides. But their legs are moving fast. Their feet strike the ground in **unison**. The crowd can't get enough of the Irish dancers.

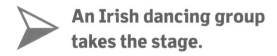
An Irish dancing group takes the stage.

A group of Irish dancers entertains a crowd.

There are two main types of Irish dancing. Some Irish dances are **social**. Others are for performance. Both began in the 1700s with dance masters. Dance masters were traveling dance teachers. They traveled among Irish villages and taught people how to dance.

The masters developed group dances. These became known as figure dances. People performed them at social gatherings called ceilis (*kay*-leez). Figure dances are performed in **formations**. Some have as few as two dancers. Others have large groups. And the steps are simple. That means anyone can learn them.

Dance masters also challenged each other to dance contests. Their solo dances are today's step dances. These dances include jigs and reels. **Hornpipes** are step dances, too. These dances require lots of skill. They can be performed solo or in groups. They can be

DANCE TIP

Don't worry about learning the steps before joining figure dances. Simply learn as you go.

 Irish dancers perform in a parade.

performed in shows for the public.

They can also be in a competition.

CHAPTER 2

DRESS LIKE YOU'RE IRISH

In group dances, costumes are based on **traditional** Irish dress. Women might wear simple dresses or skirts. The dresses feature **embroidered Celtic** designs.

Irish dancers dress in easy-to-move clothes.

A **brooch** is pinned at the shoulder.
It secures a cape.

Men wear **kilts** or pants. They
also wear jackets. The jacket
has a folded cloak draped from
the shoulder.

Step dancers wear soft shoes for
reels and jigs. For other dances,

DANCE TIP

Wear layers when performing in
an Irish ceili. You can peel off the layers
as you heat up.

 Soft shoes are easier to move in for reels and jigs.

hard shoes are better. Hard
shoes have toe tips. Their heels
are hollow. The design accents
the sounds of the footwork in
hornpipes. For figure dances, it's
best to wear leather-soled shoes.
They let dancers glide on the floor.

CHAPTER 3

STEPS AND FIGURES

Irish step dances are performed on the balls of the feet. They require good **stamina**. You must be able to kick high. Your footwork must be precise. You need to move at a fast pace. Posture is important, too.

 Irish dance takes a lot of hard work.

Your upper body should be upright.
You must also keep your arms by
your sides.

Figure dances are the traditional
dances of Ireland. They are more
relaxed. Their steps are usually
easier than those in step dancing.

DANCE TIP

In step dancing, arms are
carried close to the sides with fists
closed. Try holding a coin in each
hand to remind yourself to keep your
fists closed.

 A dancer performs at the World Irish Dancing Championships.

 Irish dance can be done alone or in groups.

Figure dances have names such
as the Bonfire and Haymakers' Jig.
Fairy Reel and the Siege of Ennis
are figure dances, too.

Another type of dancing is called *sean-nós* (*shan*-nohs). It is a traditional style of solo dancing. The step is relaxed and low to the ground. This makes it similar to tap dancing. Dancers make up the moves as they keep time to the music. The footwork is called battering. Sean-nós dancers originally danced on wooden doors or barrel tops. This is why today's sean-nós dances are still performed in small spaces.

IRISH JIG

An Irish jig starts with the left foot pointed forward.

1. Step forward onto the left foot. Bring your right foot in behind it.
2. Shift your weight to your right foot. Now bring your left toe up to your right knee as you hop.
3. While hopping, kick your left foot out in front of you.
4. Take four steps back, starting with your left foot. The fourth step ends on your right foot. This lets you point your left foot forward and start again.

An Irish jig can lead to more advanced moves.

CHAPTER 4

ON WITH THE SHOW!

In 1994, there was a popular song contest in Dublin, Ireland. A group of Irish dancers performed during **intermission**. Riverdance took off from there. A full-length show began in Dublin the next year.

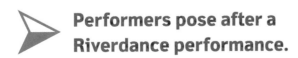
Performers pose after a Riverdance performance.

It helped make Irish dancing popular around the world.

Riverdance features upbeat music and dance. Dancers perform their steps in unison. It's hard to take your eyes off them. But Irish dancing doesn't have to be so formal. And you don't need to be

DANCE TIP

To keep a good posture, pull your shoulders back and down. Don't forget to relax.

 Irish dancing is common at Saint Patrick's Day celebrations.

Irish, either. Anyone can join the fun of an Irish social dance. It's as simple as finding a local ceili. Most Irish towns host ceilis in the summer. They welcome visitors.

 Irish dancing is a fun way to spend time with friends.

But ceilis can also be found outside Ireland. An Internet search will help you find them.

Irish dancers also compete. Competitions usually feature step dancing. To learn step dancing, you can contact your local dance studio. Most dancing schools today offer some type of Irish dance lessons.

DANCE TIP

There are many Irish dance videos online to help you master basic steps.

FOCUS ON
IRISH DANCE

Write your answers on a separate piece of paper.

1. Write a sentence that explains the main idea of Chapter 2.

2. Would you be more interested in learning step dancing or figure dancing? Why?

3. How many kinds of shoes are worn in Irish step dancing?
   - **A.** one
   - **B.** two
   - **C.** three

4. What kinds of dances would be most common at an Irish social gathering?
   - **A.** figure dances
   - **B.** step dances
   - **C.** sean-nós

5. What does **accents** mean in this book?

*Their heels are hollow. The design **accents** the sounds of the footwork in hornpipes.*

    A. makes something louder

    B. makes something slower

    C. makes something softer

6. What does **posture** mean in this book?

***Posture** is important, too. Your upper body should be upright. You must also keep your arms by your sides.*

    A. the amount of time a person dances

    B. the length of a person's arms

    C. the position of a person's body

Answer key on page 32.

GLOSSARY

brooch
A piece of jewelry pinned to clothing and worn as a decoration.

Celtic
Having to do with the cultures of Ireland, Scotland, and Wales.

embroidered
Having designs sewn onto a piece of cloth.

formations
Arrangements of people in groups.

hornpipes
Lively dances that were a favorite of sailors.

intermission
A pause in an activity such as between acts of a play.

kilts
Skirts that reach the knees, often worn by Irish or Scottish men.

social
Having to do with activities involving other people.

stamina
The ability to continue working for a long time.

traditional
Well established within a group of people.

unison
At the same time.

TO LEARN MORE

BOOKS

Foley, Catherine E. *Step Dancing in Ireland: Culture and History*. Burlington, VT: Ashgate, 2013.

Rudolph, Janice Clark. *Ireland*. New York: Bearport Publishing, 2018.

Tieck, Sarah. *Dancing*. Minneapolis: Abdo Publishing, 2013.

NOTE TO EDUCATORS

Visit **www.focusreaders.com** to find lesson plans, activities, links, and other resources related to this title.

INDEX

Answer Key: 1. Answers will vary; 2. Answers will vary; 3. C; 4. A; 5. A; 6. C